SWING

J.A. Henderson
Illustrated by Paul McCaffrey

OXFORD

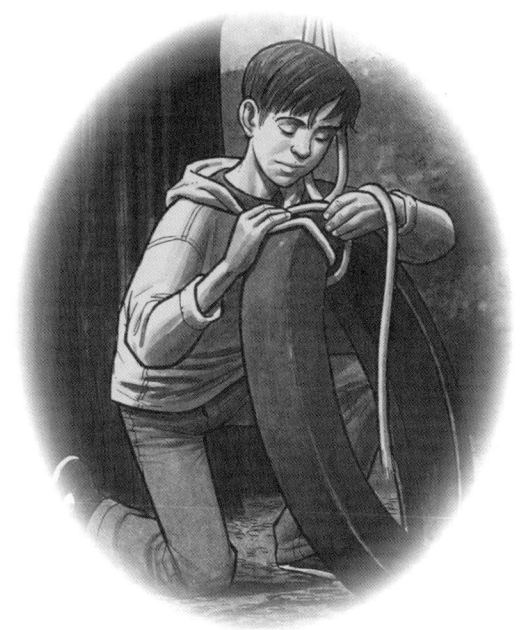

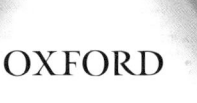

Chapter 1

I hate school holidays.

See, I live on a farm at the edge of the ocean, so the wind blows all the time and the vegetables in our garden taste like they've been dipped in salt. The nearest village is ten miles away and so are all the children.

It's not so bad during term time because I get driven to school and can hang with my mates. And, call me weird, but I *like* learning stuff. But I'm too far out for anyone to visit much during holidays and my parents treat me like one of the farm hands. So, I was anticipating three weeks of boredom interrupted by periods of hard labour.

I certainly wasn't expecting to change the universe.

Funny how things work out.

It all started with a tyre. For some reason farms always have them lying about. In fact, farms have all sorts of things lying about. You'd think my dad would tidy up a bit, but he says he's too busy trying to put food on the table. I pointed out that it shouldn't be too difficult to put food on the table when we're surrounded by animals and crops. He just snorted.

"There's some rope in the barn," he said. "Why don't you grab a tyre and go build yourself a swing?"

I asked if he had ever *heard* of computer games.

"Or you could help me milk the cows."

I decided that building a swing wasn't such a bad idea after all.

I knew just where to put it. There's a hollow with a big oak tree about half a mile from the farmhouse, surrounded by low hillocks that shelter it from the sea wind. It's also a great place to hide from my parents when they're looking for me to chop turnips or whatever.

The swing wasn't as easy to build as I'd hoped because the tyre kept hanging squint. It was getting dark by the time I finally got it right and I could hardly see my hand in front of my face.

I should have gone home right then. After all, how much fun could a swing be in the dark? But it had taken me all day to build and I was determined to try it out properly.

I should have gone home. Then everything would have been all right. But instead I climbed onto the tyre and rocked slowly, whistling to myself and feeling a bit silly.

Then I saw lights racing across the night sky, heading straight towards me.

And nothing would ever be the same again.

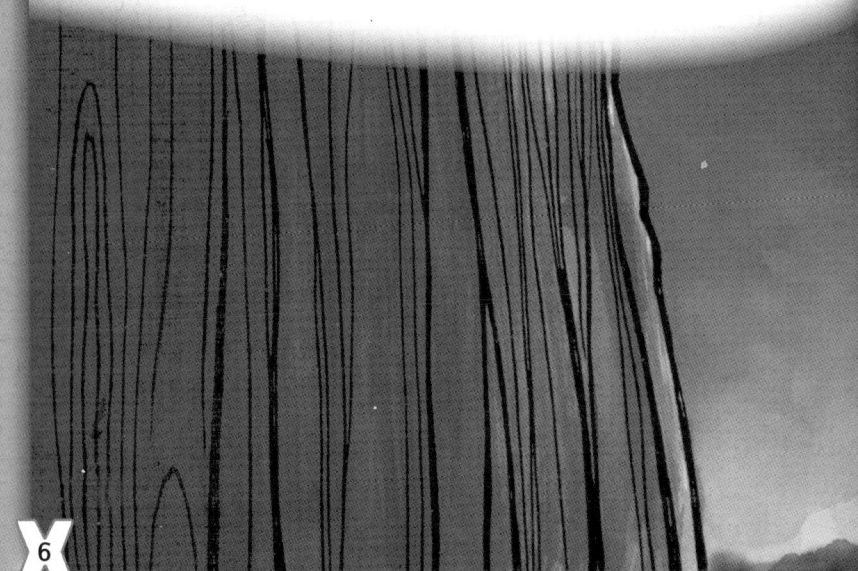

Chapter 2

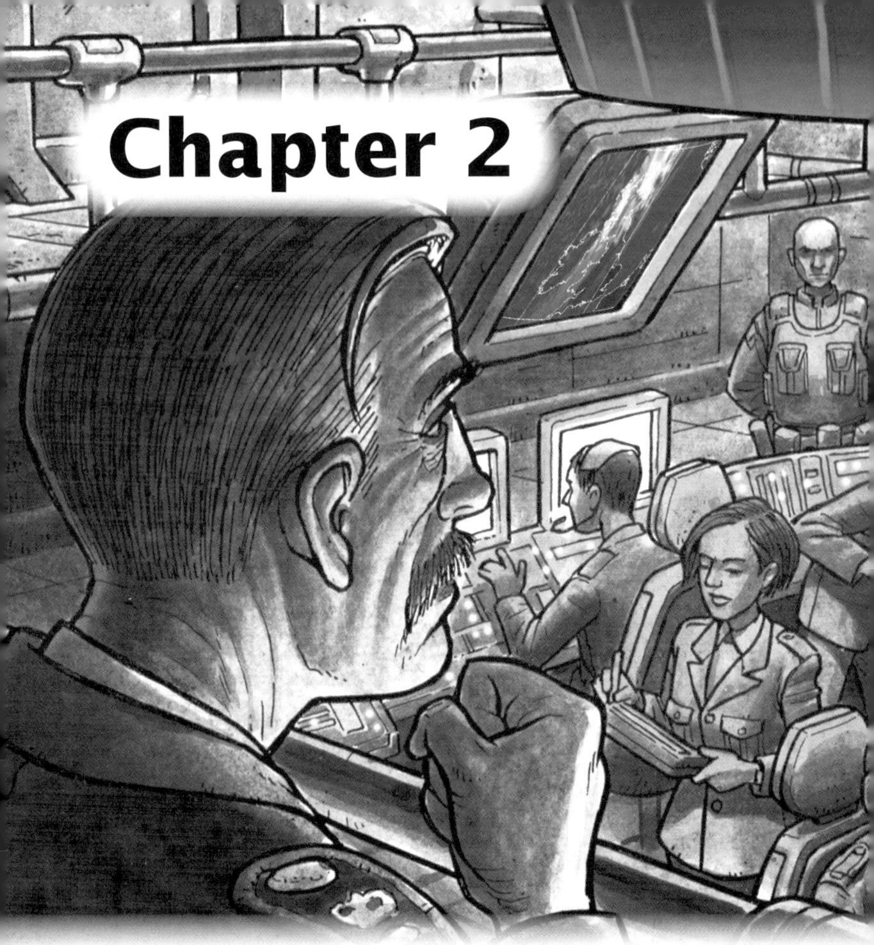

Command Centre 4 was buzzing with urgent voices. At a horseshoe-shaped console, soldiers were typing and whispering into headsets.

Colonel Reardon strode into the room, half shaved and buttoning up his tunic.

"Status report," he barked, wiping the lather from his cheeks.

"We've got unidentified objects approaching the west coast." A white-faced Lieutenant pointed to the huge screen on the wall. "Satellite's tracking them."

On the screen several red dots were moving slowly towards a section of coastline.

"What are they and where did they come from?"

"We don't know. They just ... appeared."

"That's not good enough," Reardon snapped. "Are they missiles? Are they planes?" He glared around the room. "Are they little green men from Mars?"

"Can't tell," the Lieutenant insisted. "They're moving too fast to get a visual."

"Scramble the nearest air base and get me HQ."

The Colonel held out his hand for a secure phone, eyes fixed on the screen. Then he froze, the device inches from his mouth.

The dots had reached the coastline and vanished.

Chapter 3

I stood on the tyre, still swinging. A mass of dark objects roared towards me, trailing fiery tails. I was too astonished to even jump off. Then there was a blinding flash and I fell backwards off my makeshift swing.

I pressed my face into the grass, whimpering in terror. But, after a few minutes it was obvious that I wasn't dead, just a bit muddy – so I got up and raced home. My legs were shaking so badly and the night was so black that I fell a dozen times.

When I got in, my parents were watching television with the curtains closed. Typical.

"Have a nice day, son?" Mum frowned at my dirty clothes.

"I built a swing and got attacked by a bunch of nuclear missiles," I replied, as nonchalantly as I could. "Or it might have been an alien invasion."

"Who said life on a farm was boring?" Dad took a sip of his tea. "And you've got feeding the pigs to look forward to first thing tomorrow."

"I can hardly bear the excitement."

I ate the dinner Mum had kept warm for me in the oven and went to bed.

Chapter 4

"What am I looking at here?" In the Command Centre, Colonel Reardon leafed through a sheaf of photographs.

"Infra-red satellite pictures of the coast where the objects vanished." The Lieutenant peered over his commander's shoulder. "No explosions. No damage. No debris."

"If you're telling me what we saw was a computer glitch in one of the world's most expensive defence systems, I'll be less than happy."

"Happier than if the whole place had gone up in flames?" the Lieutenant ventured.

Colonel Reardon treated him to a formidable glower.

"We don't have an explanation." The Lieutenant shook his head. "We've never seen anything like it before."

Chapter 5

Next day, after feeding the pigs, I went to check on the swing.

The tyre hung motionless from the oak tree like an oily black tear. The land around it was untouched. I began to wonder if I had imagined last night.

I sat on the tyre to think and began swinging back and forwards, watching the sun race across the cloudless sky.

Wait a minute, I thought. *You can't see the sun race across the sky. It doesn't move that quickly.*

I dug my heels into the ground and the swing stopped. The sun was suddenly back in its original position. I started again. The sun flashed over my head, sank and darkness fell like a theatre curtain. I dug in my heels and it was day again.

Now that's a bit odd, I thought to myself.

I think I was in shock.

I don't know how many times I repeated the process but the results were certainly interesting. No, *interesting* isn't the right word. *Mind-boggling* is the right word.

The faster I swung, the quicker the sun shot across the sky. Night and day passed like cards, shuffled by some invisible giant. If I swung hard enough, time actually seemed to accelerate. The world beyond the tyre and the tree became a blur of alternating blackness and light.

This time, instead of digging in my heels, I let the swing slow down naturally. Day and night stopped flashing past and I could see that the low hillocks around me were covered in snow.

Well, *that* was unexpected.

The swing came to a halt and the snow vanished. Everything was just the way it had been when I got on the tyre.

This time I walked home. My legs were trembling too much to run.

My parents were in the kitchen.

"Do anything interesting today, dear?" Mum asked pleasantly.

"I think I invented a time machine." I got some orange juice from the fridge. "Only, I'm still figuring out how it works."

"Excellent!" Dad poured himself a drink and smiled. "We forgot to send your gran a birthday card last Tuesday. Think you can nip back a week and post one?"

"At the moment it only goes forward in time." I took the juice and headed for my bedroom. "I'm still working on it."

Chapter 6

Inventing a time machine should be pretty exciting, even if you did it by mistake. But I like to keep a cool head. Besides, I couldn't figure out how it was going to be any use to me. Not if I couldn't get off the stupid tyre and actually explore the future.

That was the problem. Every time the swing stopped I returned to the present. What good was that? It was like having the keys to the world's biggest toy store and discovering the place didn't have a door.

And then it came to me. I believe it's called 'thinking outside the box'.

Whenever the swing stopped I was returned to the present. But what if I wasn't on the swing when it came to a halt?

It was worth a try.

I got on the tyre and began to swing. Days, nights, seasons, maybe even years raced past in a haze. At the swing's highest arc, I jumped off. I rolled and sprang to my feet, just like I'd seen paratroopers do in movies.

The tyre was still swinging, but the shout of triumph died in my throat.

The oak and the tyre were untouched but the hillocks around me were scorched and bare. I raced up the largest one to a spot where I could see the farmhouse.

It was gone. All that was left were a few ruined stones in the midst of a blackened, deformed landscape.

I glanced back at the swing in time to see it slow to a stop.

And suddenly my parent's farm was back. There was a wisp of smoke rising from the chimney. Green fields stretched into the distance. Corn waved gently in the sea breeze.

I ran back to the tyre and climbed on, my heart hammering. This time I swung longer before I leapt off.

The nightmarish vista hadn't changed. I ran up the devastated hill, devoid of greenery. I saw the same sight – acres of windswept, ruined land.

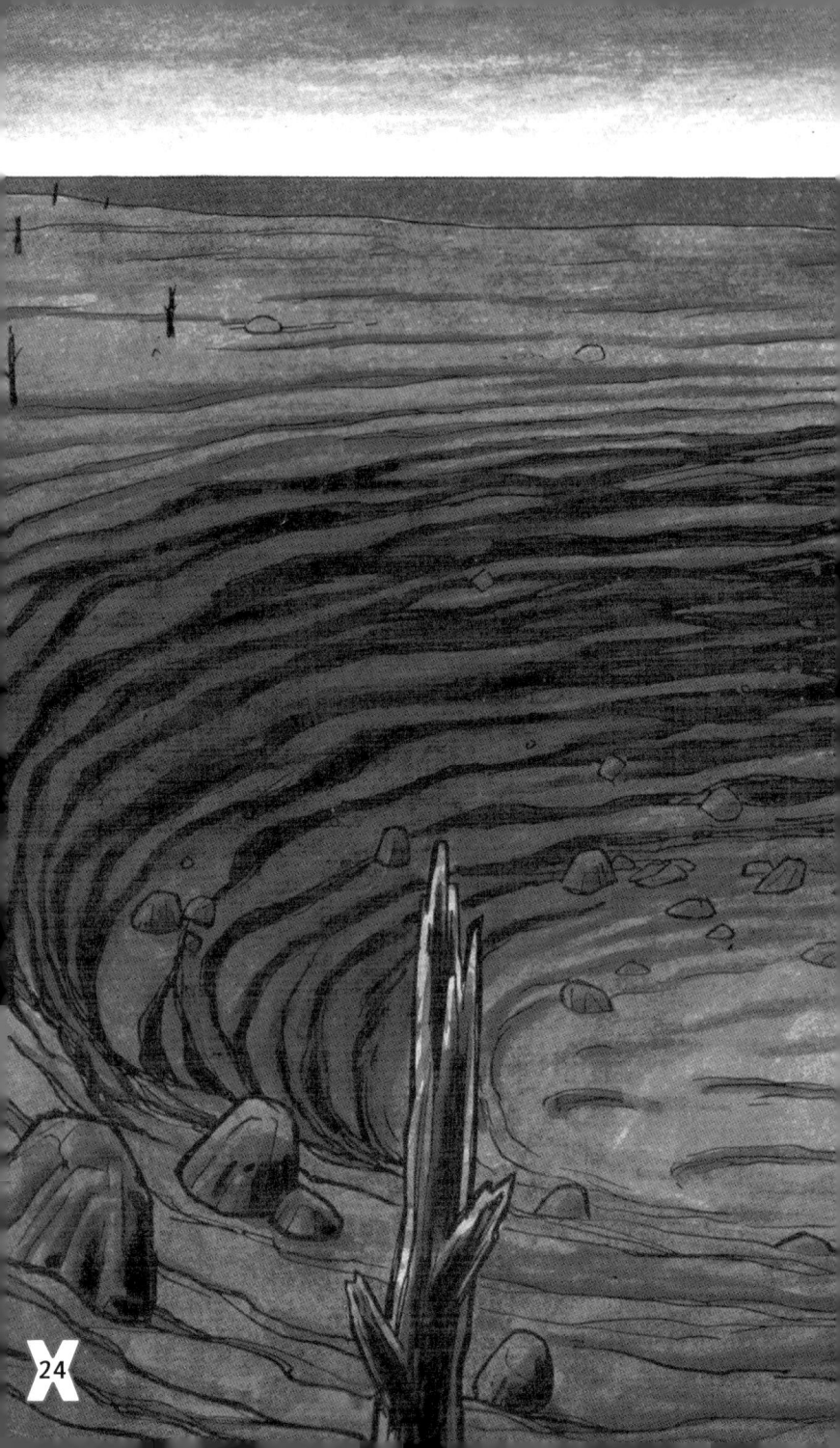

I sat down and watched the swing slow and halt. As soon as it stopped I felt grass under my hands and everything was normal again. Everything except my thoughts.

When I got home, Mum and Dad were playing cards in the living room.

"Haven't seen much of you the last couple of days." Mum peered secretively at her hand. "Want to play?"

"I think there's going to be a war." I tried to keep the tremor from my voice. "Or some kind of terrible disaster."

"You OK, son?" Dad got up and put his arm round me, shooting Mum a puzzled look. "You want a sandwich?"

"I'm not really hungry." I shrugged off his hand. "I think I'll just go to bed."

What else could I say to them?

Chapter 7

In the Command Centre, Colonel Reardon opened a brown folder marked TOP SECRET. Inside was a letter. Pulling a sheet of paper from the envelope he read it without speaking. Then he read it again.

"When was this sent?"

"It was posted weeks ago. Addressed to the headquarters of Defence and Security." The Lieutenant shrugged. "Nobody paid much attention until the last attack happened – exactly when the letter said it would." He glanced at the giant screen. It showed a shattered coastline, empty of life.

"So what does it mean?" The Colonel snarled. "Is it a threat?"

"You read the letter, Sir." The Lieutenant had dark rings under his eyes. "It's not worded like a threat. More of a prediction."

"And who the heck sent it?"

"The authorities have the letter writer in custody now. He's being questioned as we speak."

"Is he part of any hostile group?"

"Our security people have checked him thoroughly and he's clean. They can't understand how he knew what was going to happen."

The Lieutenant hesitated.

"He's just an ordinary teenager."

Chapter 8

Next day I dragged my dad to see the swing. I didn't tell him why. I figured the only way he'd believe me was if he saw it with his own eyes.

"Ah, this takes me back," he said, rocking back and forth on the tyre. To my annoyance, he stayed steadfastly in the present.

"You'd be surprised," I muttered crossly. I tried it out myself, swinging with all my might. My father watched, hands in his pockets. Nothing changed. Nothing at all.

"That's a fine show of acrobatics, son, but I have work to do." He waved a cheery goodbye and turned back for the farm. "Try not to land on your head."

Great. Somehow my dad's presence stopped this little set-up from working. Only I knew that disaster was coming and I had no way to prove it. How could I get my parents to leave the place they had worked so hard to make a home? I didn't even know when the farm would be destroyed. Time had passed so quickly on the swing that I couldn't measure it.

I had to go and see if things got better or worse. To try to find some kind of explanation. I climbed on the tyre and began to swing. I must have made a dozen trips, each time going a little further into the future. Each time jumping off when the swing was at its highest arc.

And each time, what I found was worse. A no-man's-land of churned earth and blackened stumps – great patches of soil fused by intense heat into a black, glassy mass. But my knowledge of this terrible world was restricted to how far I could run before the swing halted.

Eventually I gave up and went home.

My parents were poring over a big black book.

"I was cleaning out the attic," Mum held up the heavy volume, "and found our old photograph albums. It's got pictures of us on holiday at Loch Ness when you were a baby and all sorts of other stuff."

"I don't suppose you want to see?" Dad asked half-heartedly.

"Yes. I'd like that." I came and sat down next to them. "I'd like that a lot."

My parents looked astonished.

Chapter 9

In Command Centre 4, General Oswald Marek checked the clock on the wall. He had replaced Colonel Reardon four years ago when the operation became too important for someone of a lower rank to command it.

He turned to Dr Wilson, the new addition to base personnel. Wilson wasn't military and he wasn't under the General's direct command. Marek didn't like that at all.

Dr Wilson was looking at the time, too. The men at the consoles held their breath.

"Nothing so far," the General tutted.

"Just keep watching." The doctor nodded at the massive screen.

"There!" A soldier pointed. "There he is!"

"Where did he come from?" the General gasped.

The satellite image showed a boy standing by an oak tree. They were the only living things in the desolate landscape. The child sank to the ground and put his head in his hands. Moments later, he vanished.

"It's him all right," the General whispered. "Just like you predicted."

"Seeing is believing, Sir." The doctor put his hands calmly behind his back. "It will be exactly two years and six days until he appears again."

"Then we'll be ready."

"What do you intend to do?"

"We're going to grab him." The General gave a decisive sniff. "This has gone on long enough, Dr Wilson."

"I couldn't agree more. But it won't work." Wilson gave a heartfelt sigh. "Nothing will work until you do things my way."

Chapter 10

I enjoy figuring things out. I have a very logical mind. After my morning chores I got out my notebook and wrote down what I knew about the swing.

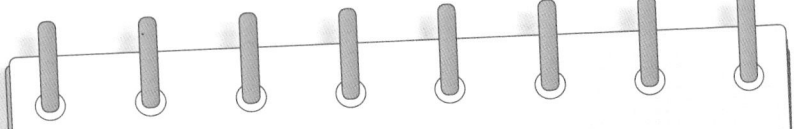

1. When I swing, I move into the future. So does the tyre and the tree.
2. But it won't work unless we're alone.
3. When the swing stops, the tyre, the tree and I immediately return to the present.
4. But if the swing is moving and I'm NOT on it, I'm able to walk around in the future till it stops. Therefore ...
5. I need to find a way to keep the tyre moving when I'm not on it.

I'm also quite good with gadgets. In the barnyard, I found an old milking pump, a truck battery, jump leads and a couple of pulleys. Thank goodness farms have so much junk lying around.

40

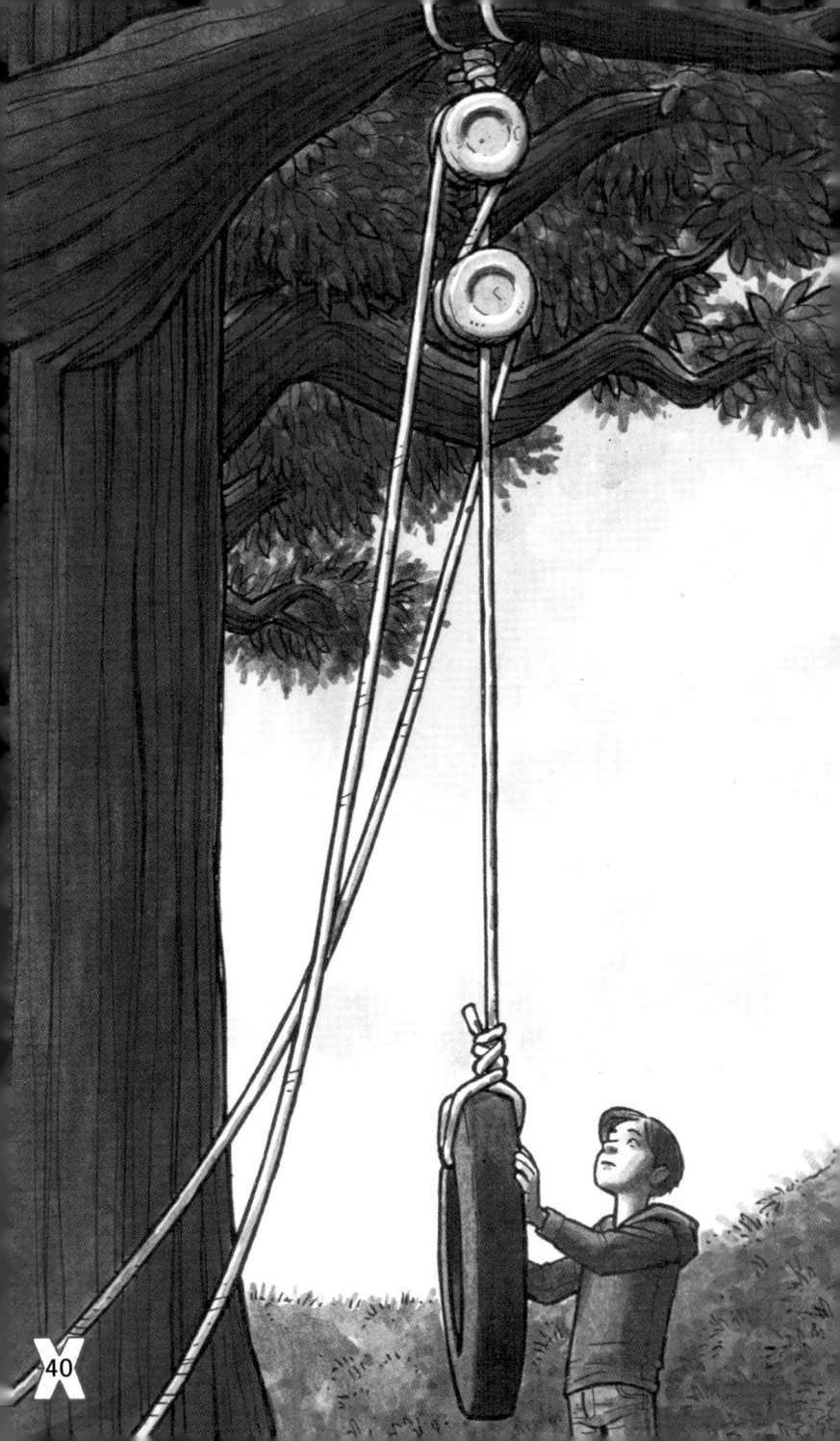

I lugged everything to the oak tree and wedged it in the fork of the largest branches.

I attached the pulleys to the ropes at the top of the swing and ran the slack through the milking pump. Then, standing on the tyre, I connected the pump to the car battery with jump leads. The shaky apparatus chugged softly and the swing began to move softly back and forwards.

It wasn't much to look at, but I was fairly confident the apparatus would stop the tyre from coming to a complete standstill once I'd jumped off.

Time to test my theory.

I kept an eye on my watch as I swung, making sure I went further into the future than ever before. Then I jumped.

I had almost become used to the desolate landscape. Almost. But this time I might be able to get far enough across it to find some clue as to what had happened. To discover why nothing had grown back, no matter how many years had gone by.

I set off in the direction of the nearest village. I was hoping in vain that it might still be there. Or I might bump into somebody who could tell me what was happening.

I had only gone a few hundred yards when the jets appeared.

Two of them swooped in from the north with ear-shredding screeches. The planes were sleek and black, a triangular design I'd never seen in any book or movie. They stopped dead and began to descend. They took only seconds to drop the two hundred feet and land on either side of me.

I turned and ran.

Glancing over my shoulder I saw ramps shoot from the underside of the planes. Soldiers poured out.

I put my head down and sprinted. My breath was coming in spurts as I leaped over lumps of twisted and fused rock, heading for my sanctuary.

The men didn't bother shouting or gesturing to each other. They ran silently and swiftly, gaining on me with every stride. I reached the hillocks and pelted down at breakneck speed.

"Stop right there, kid!" A voice shouted. "You can't outrun us."

That's what *they* thought! With a gasp I squeezed an extra burst of speed from my aching legs. A hand groped at my shoulder and slid off as I reached the tyre and slammed into it, stopping the swing dead.

I hung there for a while, panting and coughing, stopping the tyre from moving an inch.

And sure enough, when I raised my head, the soldiers and the jets were gone.

Chapter 11

In Command Centre 4 a dejected voice fizzed over the intercom system.

"We almost had him, Sir." The man sounded out of breath. "Then he reached the tree and they both disappeared."

"You were right again, Dr Wilson." General Marek folded his arms, then unfolded them again. "Next time we do it your way."

"We need to build an underground bunker." The doctor pointed to the screen. "And we need to build it where the boy always appears."

"We'll probably all die if we do." The General bristled. "That's right in the centre of the danger zone."

"Not if you build it strong enough and deep enough. You've got time." Dr Wilson looked down at his notes. "According to my calculations there won't be another attack for ten years."

He bit his lip. "But this one will be huge."

46

Chapter 12

It took me a long time to calm down. I had never considered that *I* might be in danger. What if the soldiers had caught me? Try explaining *that* to my parents.

What if there were more soldiers waiting next time?

I considered never getting back on that wretched swing again. I could untie the knots and take the tyre down right now. Be done with the whole sorry mess.

But I couldn't. I had to solve this mystery. I checked the milking pump was still working and began to swing. I'd never stayed on longer than ten minutes before. This time I stayed on for twenty. I leapt into the air.

When I landed, I finally saw something different.

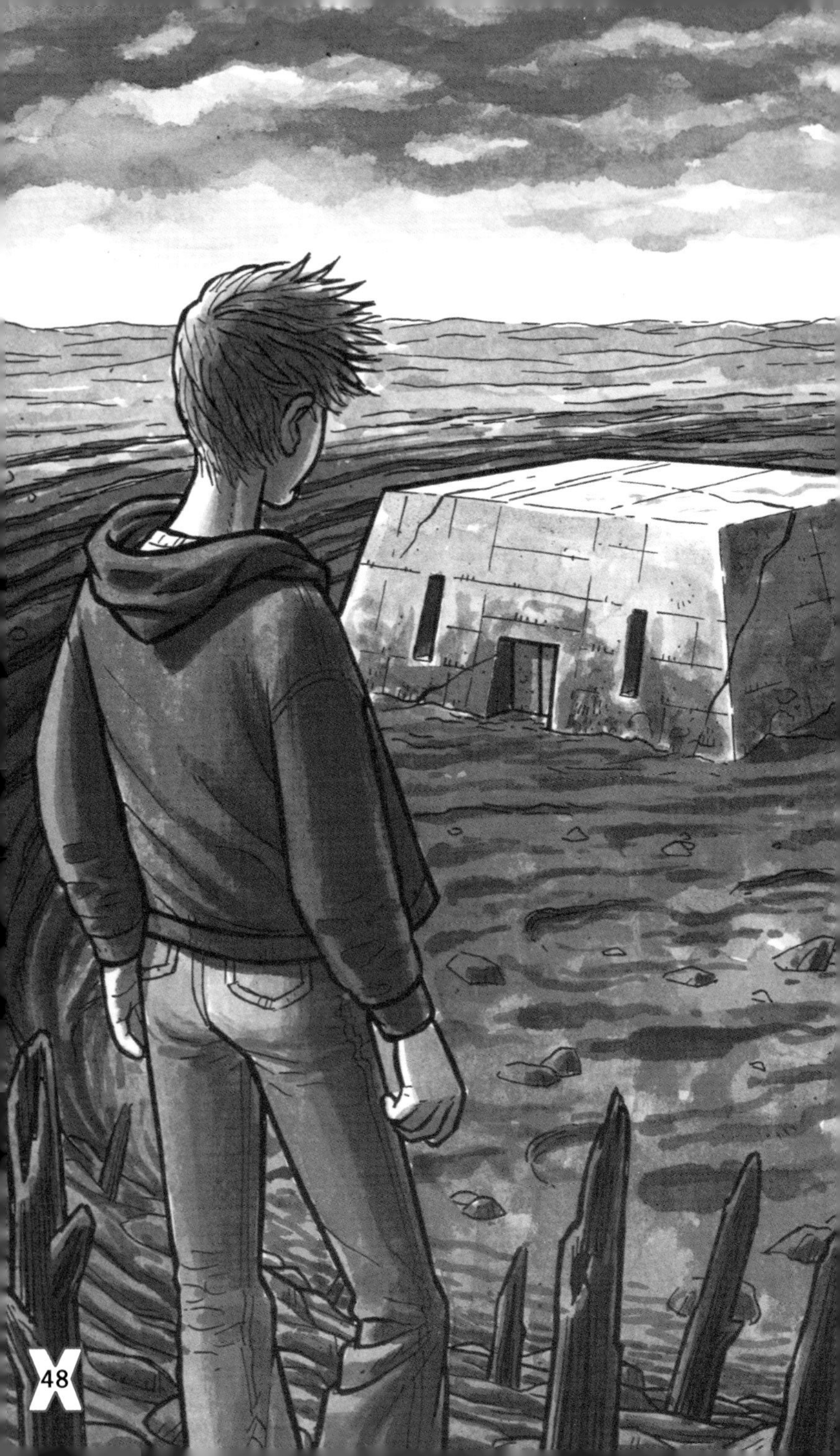

The tattered vista was still there, which didn't come as a surprise. But there was a squat concrete bunker with a steel door at the bottom of the nearest hillock. It too was black and scorched, but it wasn't in ruins.

I cautiously walked over to it, running my hands across the sooty surface. There was a hiss, the double door slid open and a man in a white lab coat stepped from the dark interior. He didn't seem surprised to see me.

I turned to dart back to the swing.

"Don't run, Sammy," the man said softly, raising his hands to show he wasn't armed. "I don't mean you any harm."

I stopped in my tracks.

"How do you know my name?" I stammered.

"I know everything about you," the man replied evenly. "Don't you recognize *me*?"

I approached him cautiously, curiosity overriding my fear. He looked to be about the same age as my dad, perhaps in his mid-forties. I had to admit he seemed sort of familiar. He had hair like mine, and green eyes like mine and thin lips like … mine.

"Yeah." The man shrugged. "My name is Dr Sam Wilson."

He gave a small bow.

"I'm you."

51

Chapter 13

"Excuse me?"

"I'm you," the man repeated. "I'm you thirty-five years from now."

"Eh … How do you do?" I didn't know what else to say.

"Not too great, if the truth be known." He nodded admiringly at the tyre, slowly chugging back and forwards. "That's very ingenious. It gives us time to have a little talk. If you don't mind, that is?"

I nodded dumbly.

Dr Wilson (I couldn't get my head round calling him anything else) sat down and patted the ground, so I joined him. He was quiet for a few seconds.

"I've heard of people talking to themselves," he chuckled. "But this is ridiculous."

I grinned back. I was relieved to see that my future self still had plenty of hair, despite being old.

"So I become a doctor?" I said hopefully. "That must pay pretty well."

"I'm a physicist." He sounded quite proud of the fact. "Actually, I'm quite famous."

"Cool!" Then I remembered why I was here. "What happened to this place?"

"You did, Sammy."

That wasn't the answer I was expecting. I waited for him to explain. Dr Wilson took a deep breath and smoothed down his coat.

"A few days ago – your time, of course – you built that swing over there."

"I did. But it's acting up a bit," I added unnecessarily.

"I know why." The doctor smiled thinly. "Just as you'd finished making it, this hollow was hit by a meteor shower. Happens all the time – 90 per cent of all meteors that reach Earth burn up in the atmosphere. This one was different.

"The meteor contained material from the very heart of the universe," he continued. "From the moment the universe began, in fact. And you, the tree and the tyre absorbed it."

Sammy gave a shudder as he remembered the dark objects with their fiery tails he had seen when he first stood on the swing.

"This meteorite material has enormous power – properties almost beyond human understanding. It can warp space and time. It enabled you to travel into the future."

"And look at what I found." I flung my arm in an arc. "Was there a war? Is it global warming?"

Dr Wilson looked at me sadly.

"The amount of energy it takes to travel through time is enormous," he explained. "You store it up as you travel into the future like a giant dynamo. But every time you leap off the swing and land you release that energy in one giant burst."

His voice dropped to a whisper. "As a massive explosion."

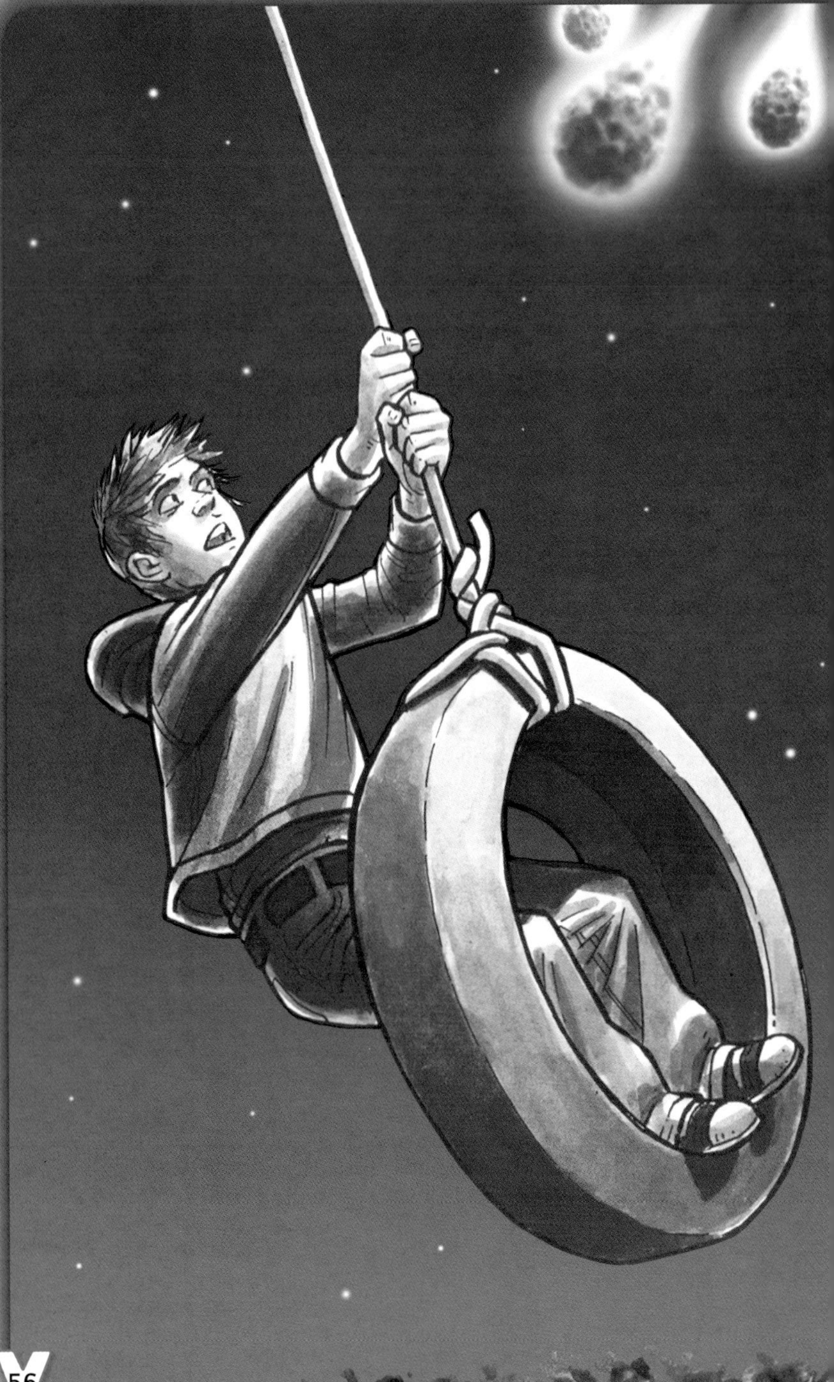

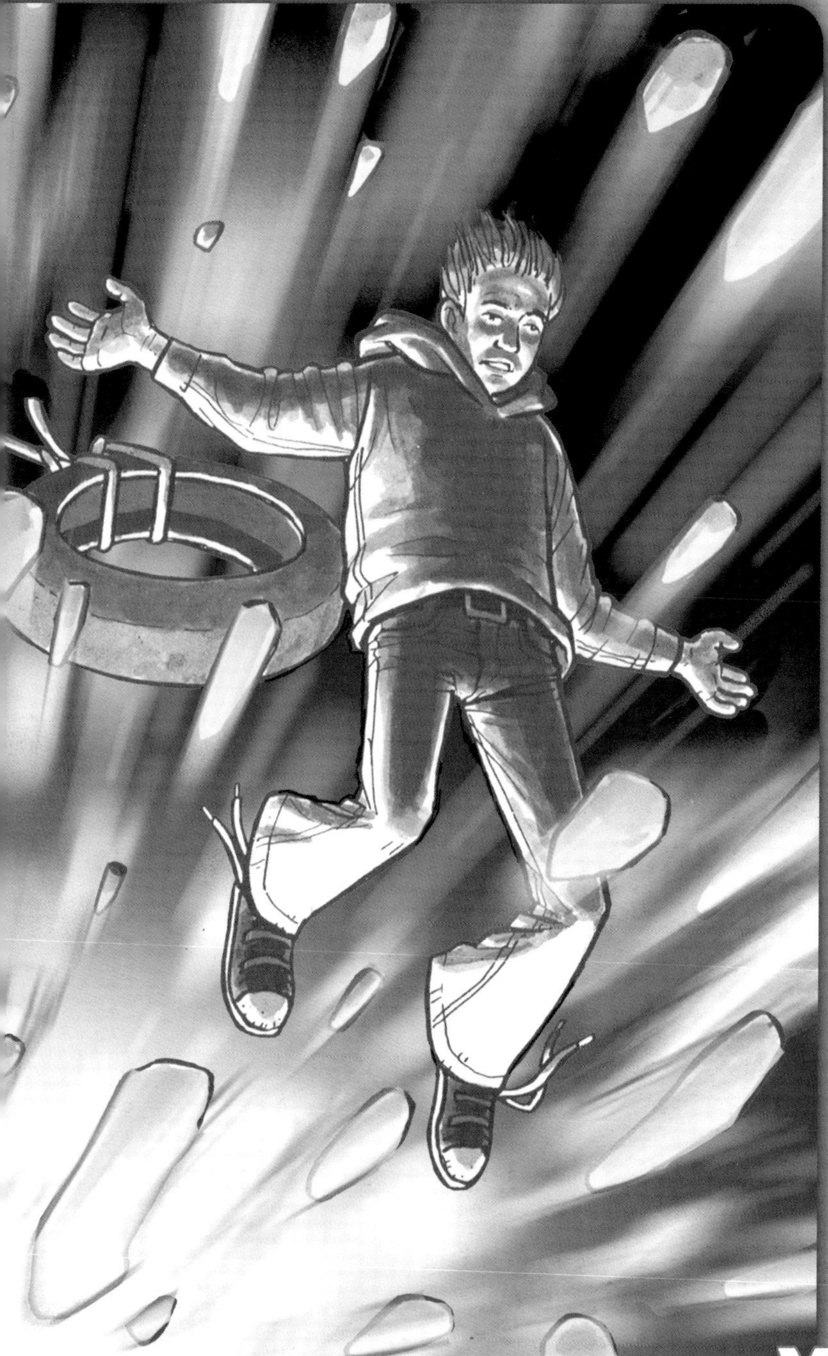

"You mean, *I* did this?" I felt panic welling up in my chest.

"I'm afraid so."

Chapter 14

My head was spinning.

"How big an area did I destroy this time?" I croaked, staring wildly around.

"You don't need to know that." The doctor laid a hand gently on my arm. "But the further you go into the future the more energy you store up and the bigger the explosion you generate."

I put a hand over my mouth.

"So no more time travel," Wilson said. "All right?"

"I'll never touch that tyre again," I replied sincerely. "Isn't there any way to reverse what I've done?"

"I'm afraid not. It's already fixed in your future and my past."

Seeing my expression, the doctor's tone softened. "Fortunately there's a way for you to minimize the damage you've caused. I need you to take this back with you."

He rummaged in his pocket and handed me a scrap of paper. "This is a list of all the dates you have appeared here over the years."

"What do I do with it?" I scanned the sheet. There were a lot of dates. I remembered with horror how many times I'd already used the swing.

"With this you'll know exactly when each explosion will occur. They're pretty small at first and cover just a few acres."

"But our parents only live a hundred yards away!"

"They don't die," Dr Wilson chuckled, tapping the top date on the paper. "Just before this first explosion you suddenly develop a burning desire to have them take you to visit Granny. After that the land is too damaged for them to ever go back."

I hung my head in shame.

"Hey!" The doctor ruffled my hair. "You save their lives, remember that."

He shivered and pulled his coat tighter around him. "When you get older, use the list. Write to the military and tell them you can predict when each explosion will occur. They won't believe you at first. They'll be convinced this is some sort of repeated enemy attack."

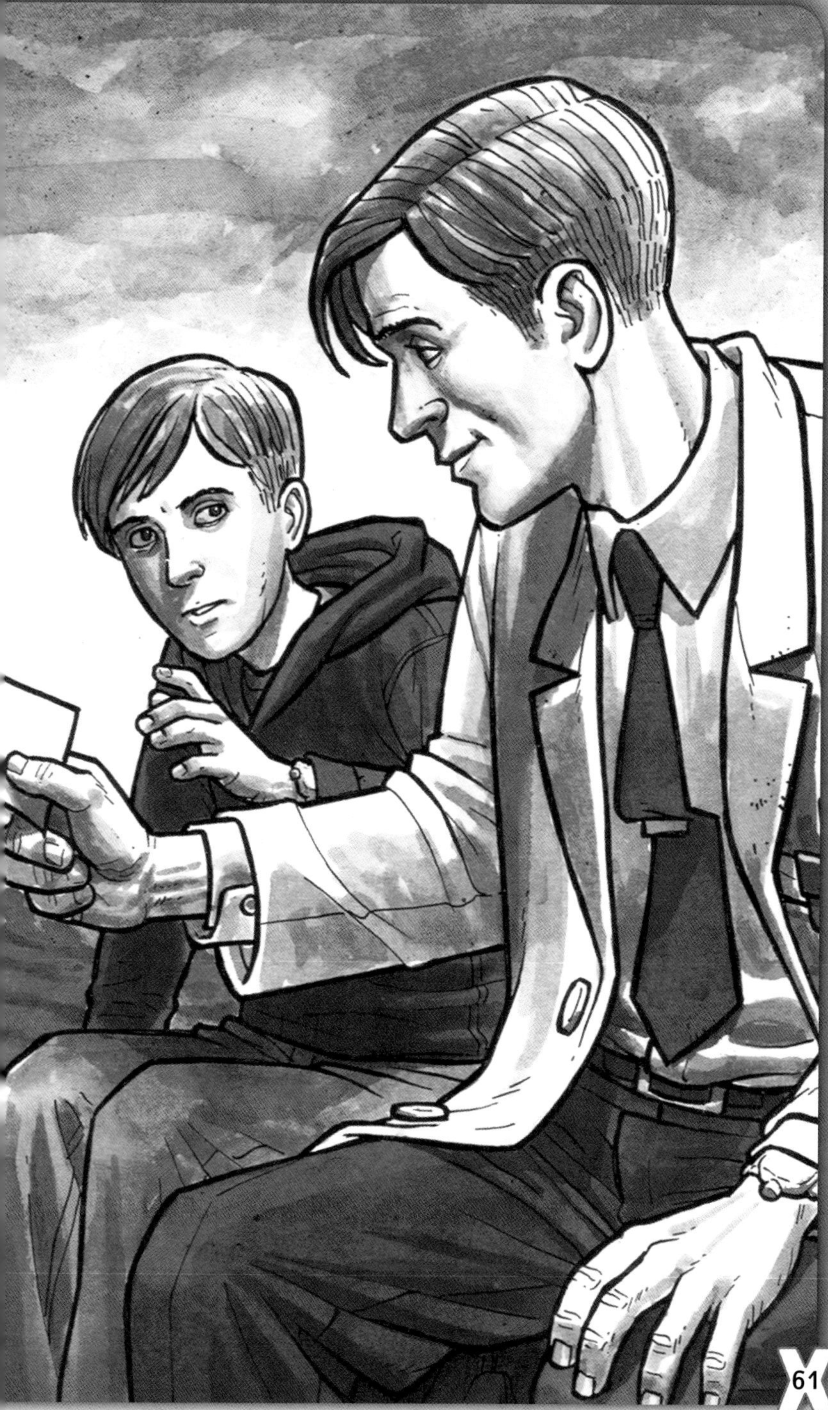

"On a deserted stretch of coastline?"

"Exactly. And when your predictions keep coming true they'll be forced to rethink." He smiled thinly. "It takes them a while. They're a stubborn lot."

"I'm not exactly going to be Mr Popular, am I?"

"No, you're not."

Wilson patted the squat concrete building beside us.

"It will take many years but, eventually, you'll convince them to build a bunker right here. One that can withstand a nuclear blast. After this explosion you'll step out and find your eleven-year-old self. Then you'll have this conversation all over again – only you'll be me this time."

I found that rather hard to get my head round. Then I had a horrible thought.

"What about this space stuff I absorbed? How do I get rid of it?"

"That's the wonderful part." Dr Wilson's eyes glittered. "You get to put it back."

He leaned over and whispered in my ear.

"Oh," I said. "Oh, my."

He gave my arm a squeeze. Then he got up and walked back to the door of the bunker.

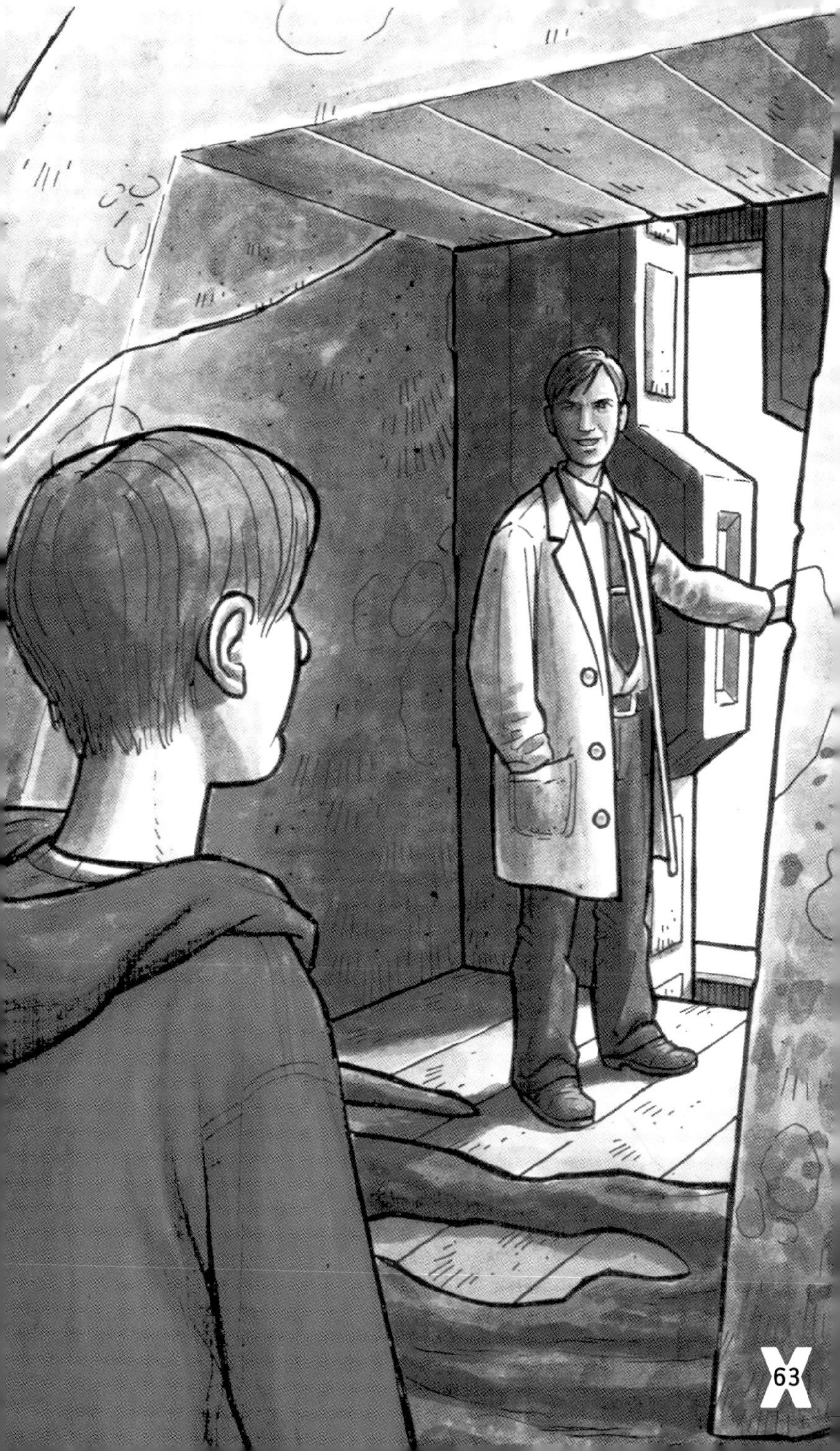

"By the way," he said casually. "You end up marrying a wonderful woman and you now have a beautiful daughter. I thought you'd like to know that."

He winked at me as the doors slid shut.

Chapter 15

Remembering what Dr Wilson had whispered to me, I got back on the tyre for my final voyage. I swung as hard and as fast as I could. I made time accelerate to an impossible speed. I stayed on for hour after hour. Though I could only see a blur, I had the sense that vast oceans of time were passing – that civilizations had risen and fallen. The ground beneath me vanished as the earth grew ancient and disintegrated. Eventually the sun exhausted itself and collapsed. Then, one by one, the stars went out.

And still I swung until the universe itself was empty. Nothing left but myself, the tyre and the tree.

Standing up on the swing, I untied the knot at the top of the first rope, just like Dr Wilson told me. It came loose and I nearly fell off. Holding tightly with one hand, I started on the other rope, the tyre spinning in wild spirals. I couldn't see in the darkness, but I could eventually feel the second knot give way.

The tree and the swing separated and I launched myself into the void.

The last thing I remember was a Big Bang – an explosion of light so bright and clean and vast that my imagination could hardly comprehend it.

And so a new universe began.

Chapter 16

I woke up in bed. My mother and father were leaning over me, relieved smiles plastered across their faces. Mum hugged me so tight I almost choked on the scent of her shampoo. My clothes were draped over the back of a chair. I could see the scrap of paper sticking up from the back of my jeans pocket.

"We found you lying in the hollow," Dad said, gingerly touching my head. "You must have fallen off the swing. You've got quite a nasty bump but you're going to be fine."

"What's kind of weird, though, is that the tyre is gone." Mum pulled at her lip. "And, er … so is the tree."

"Yes, that *is* odd," I agreed. "Am I in trouble?"

"Not at all!" Mum hugged me again. "We're just glad you're all right."

"Now that you've woken up I'm going into town to get some more bandages and chocolates and stuff." Dad stood up and put on his coat. "The doctor says you have to stay in bed for a day or two."

"You want anything else?" Mum beamed. "Maybe a book. An adventure story? Or some science fiction? You like science fiction."

I thought about all the lives I was going to have to try and save. All the questions and accusations that would come my way over the coming years. Bang went my dreams of becoming a professional footballer.

"Tell you what." I pushed myself up on the pillow and pulled my dressing gown more tightly around me.

"I wouldn't mind a book on physics."

Writing tips from J.A. Henderson

Where do you get your ideas?

I always have an eye open for interesting news articles or Internet sites. But for the most part, I just sit down and think up stories from scratch.

Where did you get the idea for this story?

I already had an idea about a whole playground where all the rides do strange things. It was very bleak and depressing and not much happened. But I did like the swing aspect. So I kept that and made it much more of a mystery story.

How do you plan your stories?

I start with an idea I like. Then I make it more complicated. I work out the beginning and end and start writing. I get stuck in the middle. So

I bring in something completely unexpected and try and make it all fit. Seems to work for me.

What do you think is important to make a good story?

Keep the reader guessing. If you can work out where the story is going next you may as well have written it yourself.

How do you create a new character?

It's like cooking. Take a bit of this and that from real characters and throw them all together. Then turn up the heat.

Do you have a routine for writing?

I usually write between 7pm and 9pm. But I'm trying to stop that. Nothing about writing should be routine.

Any other tips for creative writing?

Yeah. Enjoy it. If you don't, change the way you write until you do.

Find out more ...

For another **extreme** story, read *Volcano!*

Find out about how to survive extreme environments in *Survival Handbook*.